Tom H

GW00738532

Nice to Meet You

James Diamond

Amazon.com/author/jamesdiamond

Contents

Prologue:
Making It Big

At the time, there was no reason to expect *Big* to be a hit. Most industry insiders thought the film would be lucky to even make its money back.

For starters, *Big* would be the *fifth* comedy with this premise to be released in an 18-month period. Just as Hollywood would later have gluts of computer-generated ants or superhero team-ups, 1987-88 was the era of the age-change comedy. Dudley Moore and Kirk Cameron had swapped bodies in *Like Father Like Son* (1987); an Italian film, *Da Grande* (1987) told the story of a young boy whose wish to become an adult is granted; *Vice Versa* (1988) repeated the body-swap premise, this time with Judge Reinhold and Fred Savage; and ancient comedian George Burns became a teenager in *18 Again* (1988).

Big's script predated most of these comedies, but the film had long been stuck in "development hell."

The script was co-written by Steven Spielberg's sister Anne and her neighbor Gary Ross. At one point, Spielberg was attached to direct the script with her; his frequent collaborator Harrison Ford would have played the lead role of "adult" Josh Baskin. But Spielberg dropped out to make *Indiana Jones and the Last Crusade* (1989) and Ford took on the film's title role. *Big* had lost important star cachet.

After these losses, 20th Century Fox then handed the project to Penny Marshall, best known at the time as Laverne from the *Happy Days* spin-off *Laverne & Shirley*. Her sole previous directorial credit was the Whoopi Goldberg spy comedy *Jumpin' Jack Flash* (1986), which had been poorly received by critics and shown only mediocre returns at the box office.

Working with Marshall was not the same as working with Spielberg, and the studio had great difficulty attaching a star to the project. They were turned down by star after star—most notably by Marshall's first choice, Tom Hanks, who was too busy working on other projects. Marshall asked Kevin Costner,

Dennis Quaid, and Albert Brooks (best known today as the voice of Marlin in *Finding Nemo* and *Finding Dory*), but they all declined. John Travolta, whose career was then in a tailspin, lobbied for the part but was vetoed by the studio. Fox in turn proposed Sean Penn, who was vetoed by Marshall. Then Marshall landed a surprising coup: Robert De Niro, who at the time, and arguably still today, was considered America's leading dramatic actor. De Niro had been looking to star in something family friendly, and he had been won over by the script.

At Marshall's invitation, De Niro began spending time with the child actor who would play Josh's best friend, Jared Rushton. However, the studio surprisingly balked at casting De Niro and asked Marshall to read Warren Beatty for this part instead. She did, and asked Beatty frankly if he would be willing to take direction from her. Beatty said no, and that was that. After a story came out in a trade publication about how much family stars like John Candy and Chevy Chase were making from Fox, De Niro began having second thoughts about starring in the film as well; De Niro's proposed salary was a joke in comparison to theirs. He threatened to withdraw, but the producers would not budge. Desperate to keep him, Marshall even offered him her own salary, but De Niro quit nonetheless. He was just too angry with Fox for trying to replace him with Beatty and then refusing to give him John Candy's salary. *Big* was back in limbo.

And then Marshall had probably the best luck of her whole career: Tom Hanks's schedule opened back up, and he wanted the part.

Hanks had scored a major box office success with *Splash*, a 1984 romantic comedy that saw him opposite a mermaid played by Daryl Hannah, but since then, Hanks struggled to recapture that box office magic. He had tried acting in a spy comedy (*The Man with One Red Shoe*, 1985), buddy comedies with John Candy and Dan Aykroyd (*Volunteers*, 1985; *Dragnet*, 1987), and a marriage comedy with Shelley Long (*The Money Pit*, 1986), but the films had either been flops or resulted in very modest successes. Therefore, his agent warned him against joining a production as notoriously troubled as *Big*, but

Hanks knew it was the kind of project that could restart his career. He was in.

Hanks and Marshall were friends long before they began working on *Big*, and Hanks later credited some of the movie's magic to that pre-existing relationship; it was the first time he worked for a friend instead of beginning as someone's employee. However, that did not mean he had it easy. In fact, Hanks later described the production as the most grueling work of his career so far. Every time Marshall filmed a scene that included the "adult" Josh, she also filmed David Moscow, who played Hank's child counterpart, "young" Josh, acting out the same scene. Hanks then studied the footage in an effort to meticulously reproduce Moscow's mannerisms. He even tried to imitate Moscow's walk, which was made slightly duck-like by a recent growth spurt, and asked Marshall to provide him with poorly fitting shoes so that he could hobble when he walked, just as Moscow did. Like so many Hollywood classics, the magic and whimsy of the film's final result came at the price of exhausting labor by the cast and crew.

And then, of course, there was the piano.

FAO Schwarz had a floor piano years before a similar piano appeared in *Big*, though this piano inspired Spielberg and Ross to include a "piano dancing" moment, where Josh bonds with the CEO of the MacMillan Toys company, where he works as a data entry clerk. The interaction between Josh and Mr. MacMillan (played by Hanks's co-star Robert Loggia) propels Josh's unexpected rise to the top of the company. But when Marshall visited the store, she discovered that the existing piano would not do at all. It was only six-and-a-half feet long, and played only a single octave, making it impossible for the characters to perform a duet.

Although the piano was only needed for a minor story beat that could have been filled by any toy in the store, Marshall understood the potential of this moment and refused to give up on the script's vision. She contacted Remo Saraceni, who made the initial piano, to commission a much larger model that was sixteen feet long, with three octaves. Meanwhile, Hanks and Loggia began practicing on cardboard outlines of the piano—week after week, month after month. While the script had called for them to play only the beginner piano classic "Heart and Soul," Marshall wanted to add "Chopsticks" as well, knowing that it would be visually hilarious. Hanks recalled that the resulting rehearsals were some of the most exhausting experiences of his life, "like jumping rope for ten hours straight."

Therefore, on the day of the shoot inside of FAO Schwarz, Hanks and Loggia were surprised to arrive on the set to find two stunt doubles dressed identically to themselves. The producers had not thought that Hanks and Loggia could pull off this scene and hired two dancers to act as stand-ins. Loggia, who also played mobsters in *Scarface* and *The Sopranos*, reportedly growled at the dancers to "take a hike." Then, he and Hanks approached the piano.

The resulting scene is transcendent. With wide, dopey grins, Josh and MacMillan perform their two songs flawlessly, but by no means gracefully—they stagger, they teeter, they flap their arms in an effort to regain balance like kids pretending to be birds, but still they manage to hit their notes. Marshall films them in long, wide takes in which both actors' faces are clearly visible. A crowd forms around the two characters, exclaiming with delight at each of their leaps during "Chopsticks" and bursting into applause when they conclude their performance.

Movie audiences had a similar reaction after the film premiered. *Big* rocketed to the top of the box office upon its release, making more than $100 million, and Marshall became the first female director of a box office smash. Critics, who were prepared to savage *Big*, as they had its age-change predecessors, found themselves swooning instead at the movie's sweetness and whimsy—something movies like *Vice Versa* noticeably lack.

Most of all, *Big* vaulted Hanks ahead of contemporary comedians like John Candy or Steve Martin to be recognized as a leading actor of his generation; he received universal acclaim, and even received his first nomination for the Academy Award for Best Actor. This movie introduced an image of Tom Hanks that we hold to this day: not a slapstick artist like Chevy Chase or a laser of dramatic intensity like Al Pacino, but an "everyman" who is simple, unaffected, decent, and kind. Hanks has occasionally complained of and unsuccessfully rebelled against this "nice guy" persona, but a generation of moviegoers have defined him this way and this image has helped him create performances that will be watched by many more generations to come.

Big was only the beginning.

Chapter 1:
Early Years and *Bosom Buddies*

Thomas Jeffrey Hanks was born on July 9, 1956, in Concord, California. His mother, Janet Marylyn Frager, was a waitress, and his father, Amos Mefford Hanks, was a bookish, dreamy short-order cook with aspirations to become a writer. Tom was the third of four children. His parents' marriage was an unhappy one, however, and Janet and Amos divorced when Tom was five years old. Although it was unconventional at the time, Amos took their children, Sandra, Larry, and Tom (save Jim, the youngest, who remained with his mother).

Tom said he vividly remembered his parents' abrupt separation in later interviews; he was awakened in the night and told he had to leave with his father right away. He wanted to pack up his whole toy chest, but his father told him he could only select one or two toys to bring with him— agony for a five-year-old. Soon, the mystified children, minus Jim, settled with their father in Reno, Nevada. The divorce was not properly explained to them for months. Shortly after the divorce, Amos married Winifred Finley, a mother of eight and Tom's first stepmother. Tom and his siblings were thrust into a massive family that one of them later compared to *The Brady Bunch*. However, this marriage proved even less successful than Amos's first, and within two years, he divorced again and left just as abruptly with his children.

First Interests

Given his father's restless nature, Tom lived in ten different houses in as many years, but his father's profession may have impacted Tom's career path. Amos was far more successful in his career than he was in marriage, and made a name for himself as one of the top caterers in northern California and Nevada. Given the territory, he inevitably catered for Hollywood stars, cooking for celebrities such as Marilyn Monroe, Judy Garland, and Clark Gable. Since Tom was becoming increasingly flamboyant and dramatic, the other Hanks children, influenced by their father's brushes with stardom, began pretending that they were paparazzi following Tom into public places. Tom would then act as if he were a vain star preening for the cameras. It was a startlingly prescient game—except, of course, for the vanity.

While his father was at work, Tom watched endless hours of television and the programs he watched influenced some of the roles that he pursued or the programs that he produced later in life. Amos worked long hours so the children were often home alone for long periods of time. Amos was particularly determined to provide all of his children with a fine education and worked himself to the bone to save up for their college funds. Tom developed a particular obsession with following the Apollo program (1961-72), designed to put a man on the moon, and its progress on television. This interest led directly to Hanks pursuing roles in, or producing, some of his best-known later works, the film *Apollo 13* (1995) and the television miniseries *From the Earth to the Moon* (1998).

Similarly, in school, Tom primarily perked up when the class was about space, though he got mostly As and Bs on his report cards; despite his high marks, he said that he liked to joke around too. At school, Tom was a self-described loudmouth and class clown, but said he was careful never to push it too far: "I would only toy with authority up to the point that authority would get mad at me and then I would back off. If the teacher wasn't laughing, I'd shut up." This description is reflective of Hanks's persona in films such as *A League of Their Own* (1992) or *You've Got Mail* (1998), where his character starts off with a gruff persona, but eventually, backs down and reveals himself to be more kindhearted than other characters initially thought.

Pure Hell

In 1965, when Tom was nine years old, Amos got married again, to a Chinese American woman named Frances Wong; Tom remembers this period as a difficult time and pursued outlets that helped him to escape his home life, since the marriage proved a disaster for all involved. Wong believed in traditional Chinese culture, and while Amos hoped that this would provide his children with a useful cross-cultural experience, they quickly rebelled against this strict discipline, as well as her Chinese cooking. Tom's older siblings, Sandra and Larry, left the family after a few years and returned to living with their mother. Tom later called this part of his life "just too painful a time to remember ... pure hell."

Despite his deteriorating home situation, Tom found two important avenues of escape. He briefly became an intense, born-again Christian—"a Bible-toting evangelical" and even a "Jesus freak," in his later phrases. "A great group of people ran a church near where I lived, and they provided a safe, nurturing atmosphere at a time there wasn't much else I could count on," he said. Although Hanks later left this evangelical church and moderated his views, he recalled that this experience was "one of the best things I ever did ... Religion helped me." He became interested in film and drama with almost equal intensity. Given his obsession with space travel, he saw Stanley Kubrick's *2001: A Space*

Odyssey more than 20 times. He also appeared in his high school's plays, including Rodgers and Hammerstein's classic *South Pacific* and Tennessee Williams's *The Night of the Iguana*. When his high school's drama department gave out its "Best Actor Oscar," Tom Hanks was the recipient.

Tom in the Theater

After graduation, Hanks enrolled in Chabot College, a local community college, where he took several drama courses. Initially, he took the classes for fun, but soon he realized that his interest went deeper than a mere hobby. Instead of going to basketball games with friends, he went to plays alone: "I wouldn't take dates with me. I'd just drive to a theater, buy myself a ticket, sit in the seat and read the program, and then get into the play completely. I spent a lot of time like that, seeing Brecht, Tennessee Williams, Ibsen, and all that."

Despite his experience acting in high school plays, initially, Hanks aspired to be in a play's crew, rather than the cast; he imagined himself building sets or operating the lights. His big break came when he worked briefly at a community theater company in Sacramento. Although he built sets while at the company, he also took a supporting role in a production of Anton Chekhov's *The Cherry Orchard*. His boss, guest director Vincent Dowling, then invited Hanks to join him in Cleveland as an intern at the 1977 Great Lakes Shakespeare Festival. Hanks remembered the invitation with glee:

It's not like I went out and popped champagne— who could afford champagne? But man, I was in a car, and I was driving across the country and I had a job and I was going to be doing something that I love.

During this same year, another major change occurred, related to Hanks's love life. In 1977, Hanks and Samantha Lewes, his girlfriend and college sweetheart, had their first child. After their son Colin was born in Sacramento, the couple married the following year. During this period, the couple split their time between Cleveland and Sacramento. Hanks worked intermittently as a stagehand and carpenter for theater companies in both cities. Although he was an unpaid intern in Cleveland, he was able to support himself by winning the occasional paying, on-stage role. In 1978, he played the sinister Proteus in Shakespeare's comedy *The Two Gentlemen of Verona*, for which he won the Cleveland Critics Circle Award for Best Actor; it was one of the few times in Hanks's career that he found real success playing a villain.

Hanks and Lewes sold their car and moved to New York in 1979 because they wanted to pursue careers on Broadway. During this time, Hanks and Lewes supported themselves on unemployment. In New York, Hanks landed his first minor film role, in a shoestring-budget slasher movie called *He Knows You're Alone* (1980). The film has been utterly forgotten today save for Hanks's involvement. Hanks had only seven minutes of screen time, but it was enough to get him noticed by a talent scout for the American Broadcasting Company (ABC) television network.

Bosom Buddies

ABC flew Hanks back out to California for a series of readings, and offered him a contract that would allow them to use him in any of their shows. They were particularly interested in putting him in *Bosom Buddies*, a series that was still in development, but before then, they placed him in other roles. In early 1980, they gave him a guest-starring role on *The Love Boat,* an anthology series about a cruise ship that provided Hanks with his first chance to watch himself on television.

Later that year, Hanks filmed his pilot for *Bosom Buddies*, a sitcom in which two friends disguise themselves so that they can move into an all-female hotel; the obvious hijinks ensue. Although the series was loosely based on the comedy classic *Some Like It Hot* (1959), starring Jack Lemmon, Tony Curtis, and Marilyn Monroe, the show never came close to this illustrious predecessor. While *Bosom Buddies* began with decent ratings, those steadily fell as the show went on, perhaps in part because of several time slot changes by the network. ABC finally pulled the plug after 37 episodes, over a period of two seasons, due to these poor ratings and middling-to-above-average reviews. Critics liked the performances by Hanks and co-star Peter Scolari, but ridiculed the idea that anyone could genuinely mistake Hanks in drag for a human female and not—as one put it—a "female moose in distress."

But for Hanks, appearing on *Bosom Buddies* was a crucial debut. The show introduced his face to millions of Americans. It gave him his first steady acting paycheck, and much-needed validation. It also gave Hanks an important chance to hone his craft in front of the camera, something his previous brief appearances had never done. For example, he had only been on set for *He Knows You're Alone* for three days. He describes himself as starting out as a "lousy actor," but receiving important mentorship, as he continued to work with more experienced cast members on the set of *Bosom Buddies*.

Although being on the show helped him to improve his acting abilities, Hanks did not mind that his time on *Bosom Buddies* had come to an end. He was tired of spending his working days in women's clothing and ready to move on to new projects. As it turns out, there were plenty waiting for him.

Chapter 2:
Making a Splash

Mazes and Monsters

In 1982, Hanks landed his first leading role in a film—albeit for television—a current-events-driven piece titled *Mazes and Monsters*. In the early 1980s, the popularity of the tabletop roleplaying game *Dungeons & Dragons* had exploded, leading to a sharp cultural counter-reaction. The media hyped the games' potential connections to Satanism and when a troubled young *D&D* player named James Dallas Egbert III disappeared after his first suicide attempt, reporters were breathless. Had fellow players, who lost their ability to distinguish roleplay from reality, murdered him? Of course not—it later turned out he had just run away from home—but the story was too juicy for writers like novelist Rona Jaffe to resist exploring.

Her thinly veiled fictionalization *Mazes and Monsters* was adapted for the small screen for CBS and Hanks was cast as Robbie Wheeling, a college student who gradually goes insane playing the roleplaying game "Mazes and Monsters." Just as most people do not remember *He Knows You're Alone*, everyone, except for *Dungeons & Dragons* enthusiasts, seem to have forgotten *Mazes and Monsters* today. And though reviewers panned the movie's laughably panicked tone, Hanks's performance was again appreciated.

Hanks continued to land guest-starring roles on television, appearing several times on the sitcom *Family Ties* as the tragic, alcoholic Uncle Ned. More significantly for his future, he appeared on *Happy Days*, the sitcom that had once starred actor-director Ron Howard, who played teenager Richie Cunningham for seven years. Howard had begun his directing career before Hanks joined the cast so he did not appear opposite Hanks on the show. But he still watched it, of course, and it just so happened that he was looking for a lead for the new film he was directing—a mermaid comedy called *Splash*.

Splash

Walt Disney Studios had been working on *Splash* for a while now. Based on a script by the fabulously named writers Marc "Babaloo" Mandel and Lowell Ganz, *Splash* is romantic comedy about a mermaid who saves a man and then falls in love with him. As in Disney's later animated feature *The Little Mermaid,* the mermaid follows the man into the human world, but is unable to speak. Hijinks follow. The mermaid seeks to conceal her identity, but bumbling scientists and eventually, the US Military race to expose and capture her. In the end, the pair escape to the mermaid's undersea kingdom together.

Daryl Hannah had been cast as the mermaid, but Howard had more trouble casting the male hero and the hero's brother. The list of actors who had already refused the part is a who's who of early '80s comedy: Bill Murray, Chevy Chase, Dudley Moore, Michael Keaton, John Travolta, and Burt Reynolds. Howard brought Hanks in to read for the hero's brother at first, but he and the producers were amazed at Hanks's calm audition, and his ability to be "funny, but not quirky or eccentric"—the down-to-earth quality that would one day enthrall audiences around the world. He cast Hanks in the lead instead and cast John Candy as the brother.

Howard saw immediately how to play to Hanks's strengths. While Candy and co-star Eugene Levy (alums of *Second City Television*, a cutting-edge Canadian sketch comedy show) were both encouraged to play up their characters' humorous aspects, Howard instructed Hanks to play the straight man in most scenes. He became the film's emotional center, a relatable "everyman" in a fantastic situation. These roles would become the core of Hanks's later career.

Sweet and funny, *Splash* was a huge and unexpected success that made almost $70 million at the box office on an $8 million budget and launched the careers of all involved. Critics loved it too and it is still regarded as one of the best comedies of the 1980s. Howard, once known as little Opie Taylor on the *Andy Griffith Show* and later, for his role on

Happy Days, went on to become one of Hollywood's premier directors, later reuniting with Hanks for *Apollo 13* and the Robert Langdon movies, *The Da Vinci Code*, *Angels & Demons*, and *Inferno*. Hannah became a sensation and starred later in the decade that *Splash* premiered in acclaimed films such as *Wall Street* (1987) and *Steel Magnolias* (1989). And Tom Hanks became Tom Hanks.

Searching for a Follow Up

Although the film proved only a modest box office draw, Hanks had another success in 1984 with *Bachelor Party*, a raunchy comedy about the sexual shenanigans of a school bus driver and his friends the night before he gets married. The films' low production budget meant that it was still an important financial success that further cemented Hanks's reputation as a bankable star on the rise. Critics found Hanks to be the only worthwhile feature in the movie. As one wrote, "he's all over the place, practically spilling off the screen with an over-abundance of energy."

Hanks did not mind appearing in "dumb" films if they were all that was available and explained to one interviewer his reason for doing so: "I'm an actor. An actor has to act. What else am I supposed to do— sit around the house?" But these goofy, zany parts proved a poor bet for him in the long run, ignoring the grounded, everyday decency that is his primary asset as an actor.

Hanks followed these roles with a part in *The Man with One Red Shoe* (1985), a spy spoof co-starring Dabney Coleman, Jim Belushi, and Carrie Fisher. Hanks approached his role as a concert violinist assiduously and practiced playing the violin for five hours each day, for the better part of a year. However, he would have been better advised to spend his time polishing the film's weak jokes. Despite the previous success of *The Tall Blond Man with One Black Shoe* (1972), the French farce on which this film was based, the remake was unfunny to its core, rejected by audiences and panned by critics.

Hanks had no more luck on his next film, *Volunteers* (1985). This film reunited him with *Splash* co-star

John Candy and the two played volunteers in the United States Peace Corps. Hanks's spoiled character Lawrence Bourne III joins the Peace Corps simply to escape his creditors. The pair is assigned to Thailand, where they find themselves embroiled in a complicated plot involving innocent villagers, the CIA, and a drug lord. The film was not a debacle on the level of *The Man with One Red Shoe*, but still struggled at the box office and with critics, who were not entirely sold on Hanks's performance as the smug, spoiled lead. Today the movie is considered notable simply for putting Hanks opposite his future wife Rita Wilson, who played Beth Wexler, the female lead, though the two had also previously worked together on an episode of *Bosom Buddies*.

The Busiest Year

Hanks continued to chase the success he had glimpsed with *Splash* and in 1986, starred in three different films. The first, *The Money Pit*, was a broad comedy in which Hanks and Shelley Long (Diane from *Cheers*) played a married couple who buy a "fixer-upper" mansion, but are soon physically and financially overwhelmed by the endless repairs that threaten their marriage. Critics hated the film, often comparing it unfavorably to the 1948 Cary Grant classic *Mr. Blandings Builds His Dream House*, but it reaped modest returns at the box office.

Looking to expand out of slapstick, Hanks also agreed to do a low-budget, limited release romantic drama set in pre-World War II Palestine, where he co-starred as an American pilot in the Royal Air Force and falls for a Jewish girl of Spanish descent (Cristina Marsillach), titled *Every Time We Say Goodbye*. The lackluster film received next to no promotion, screened in few theaters, and is notable only for being one of the only films made in the Judeo-Spanish language of Ladino.

But the most significant role for him that year was *Nothing in Common*, directed by Garry Marshall, Penny Marshall's older brother. It was a dramatic rather than a comedic role, in which a young man (Hanks) must reconcile with his estranged, terminally ill father (Jackie Gleason). For the first time, Hanks's contract allowed him to have input into the film's development, and he was able to draw on his own experiences with his parents' divorce and his father's kidney disease—which caused his father to be on the brink of death a number of times— to develop his character.

Nothing in Common got mixed reviews and little box office attention, but Hanks found the experience revealing:

It changed my desires about working in movies. Part of it was the nature of the material, what we were trying to say. But besides that, it focused on people's relationships. The story was about a guy and his father, unlike, say, *The Money Pit*, where the story is really about a guy and his house.

The world may not have noticed him as a dramatic actor yet, but Hanks at last had a clear vision of where his career was headed.

New Directions

After two serious films in a row, Hanks felt he needed a break, and agreed to do *Dragnet* (1987) with *Saturday Night Live* legend Dan Aykroyd. On television, *Dragnet* had been a straight-laced, serious police procedural. However, in this reboot, Aykroyd, who played Sergeant Joe Friday, used Friday's well-known "Just the facts, ma'am" catchphrase for laughs, while Hanks played Friday's modern, streetwise partner Detective Pep Streebek. The film was a modest hit, but Hanks and Aykroyd proved less than the sum of their parts as a comic duo. Hanks began to cast around for a part that would take him in a new direction.

Meanwhile, his personal life was also in upheaval. The same year that *Dragnet* was released, Hanks divorced Lewes, his wife of nine years. Hanks generally declines to speak about the divorce in interviews beyond saying that they had simply married too young. The couple had two children, Colin, and Elizabeth, who had been born in 1982. Recalling his own experiences after his parents' divorce, Hanks worried greatly about how the split would affect them. Although he had a busy filming schedule, he worked hard to remain a large part of their lives.

Despite his newly single status, Hanks avoided the usual Hollywood route of making the rounds with various models and starlets; he had already lost his heart to Rita Wilson. Initially, the two met when Wilson appeared in an episode about a video dating service on *Bosom Buddies*. Then, despite still being married to Lewes, Hanks said that he fell for Wilson while co-starring with her on the set of *Volunteers*. The two married the year after his divorce from Lewes and have remained together ever since. They also have two children: Chester, who was born in 1990, and Truman, who was born in 1995. Later, Hanks described his relationship with Wilson in an interview with Oprah that was published in the 2001 issue of *O, The Oprah Magazine*:

When I married Rita, I thought, 'This is going to require some change on my part.' I won't deny that providence was part of us finding each other, but our relationship isn't magic – the way it's shown in movies. In real life, our connection is as concrete as me sitting here. Not that marriage doesn't come close to being hell in a handbasket sometimes. But we both know that no matter what, we'll be with each other – and we'll get through it.

And then, finally, after all of these changes in his personal life, the part Hanks had been looking for fell right into his lap. It was the perfect blend of dramatic and comedic—just funny enough that the producers supported him, but requiring enough acting chops so that he could use it to launch a whole new direction for his career. The name of the movie that allowed Hanks to play this part was *Big* (1988).

Chapter 3: Best Actor

Failures

After the runaway success of *Big,* Hanks made an attempt to break out of his "nice guy" image with a role as an unpleasant stand-up comic in *Punchline* (1988). It was not a success. The film received only mixed reviews from critics, and failed to make a mark at the box office.

Things got worse. Hanks had signed a multi-picture deal with Disney Studios, but these productions were generally troubled. As biographer David Gardner observes, Hanks seemed to be unable to say "no" in his first decade in movies, and as a result, got involved with many films he should have avoided.

A prime example was *The 'Burbs* (1989). Audiences were eager for another comedy from Hanks, and Disney could not wait to supply them with one. Joe

Dante (of *Gremlins* and *Innerspace*) directed the film, in which Hanks and Carrie Fisher played suburbanites whose neighbors may or may not be crazed serial killers. Hanks and other neighborhood residents investigate, leading to a series of slapstick falls and supposedly comical misunderstandings. Unfortunately, it just was not funny, and despite a record opening weekend, the film's numbers then plummeted under the weight of poor word-of-mouth.

Later that year, *Turner & Hooch* did much better, despite a troubled production in which Hanks reportedly clashed with the film's initial director, former *Happy Days* star Henry Winkler ("The Fonz"). Roger Spottiswoode replaced Winkler after a few weeks, but the film was already crippled by being behind schedule. The story is not much—a large, lovable, destructive dog ("Hooch") is the only witness to a homicide, and neatnik Detective Turner (Hanks) must reluctantly adopt him while chasing the bad guys. But Hanks's charm, and his surprising chemistry with his French Mastiff co-star, managed to raise the film to at least mediocrity, and it was financially successful.

There was every reason to believe that Hanks's next film *Joe Versus the Volcano* (1990) would be a success. Its writer and director, John Patrick Shanley, had just won an Oscar in 1988 for his *Moonstruck* (1987) screenplay. Later, in 2004, his play *Doubt: A Parable* would become one of the most acclaimed dramas of the young century. But even a genius can misfire, and *Joe Versus the Volcano* proved to be a hodgepodge of entertaining elements that never quite gelled. Hanks played Joe, a hypochondriac, who is persuaded by a corrupt doctor that he has a lethal "brain cloud"; he therefore accepts a billionaire (Lloyd Bridges's) suspicious offer to live in luxury for a short period of time before he must leap to his death into a volcano, allowing the billionaire to appease the island's natives and claim important mineral rights. Along the way, he romances three women, all of them played by Meg Ryan. Audiences and critics alike were befuddled, and the movie flopped.

Bonfire

Hanks was not as troubled as he might have been by the failure of *Joe Versus the Volcano*, in part because he had just learned that he landed a dream role: Sherman McCoy in *The Bonfire of the Vanities* (1990).

Bonfire was one of the bestselling novels of the decade, a satire of New York City politics by journalist-turned-novelist Tom Wolfe. In it, McCoy, a fabulously wealthy bond trader, is out one night with his mistress when two black youths appear to threaten them; the mistress drives McCoy's car into one of the teenagers, putting him in a coma. The police uncover McCoy's involvement, a reporter fans the flames, and the ambiguity of the youths' intentions makes the case a *cause célèbre* and racial flashpoint for the entire city.

There were immediate concerns among the novel's fans that the sympathetic "everyman" Hanks was the wrong choice for the shallow, avaricious McCoy. But with Brian De Palma (*Scarface*, *The*

Untouchables) directing, and a cast including Hanks, Bruce Willis, Melanie Griffith, and Morgan Freeman, *Bonfire* was anticipated to be the next *Gone with the Wind*. Hanks could not say no.

Instead, it was one of the all-time great Hollywood flops. Hanks was poorly suited to his role, and Willis was even worse in his—which, amazingly, had originally been intended for John Cleese. De Palma and the screenwriter had made major changes to the novel, all of which were poorly received by its many fans. The movie all but disappeared from the box office on its release, and lost tens of millions of dollars.

Foreshadowing the words of his most famous character, Hanks said at the time that when making a movie, you could never quite tell what you were going to get:

It feels just the same when you're filming a hit or a flop... who would have thought audiences would break into applause at me dancing on a big piano keyboard in *Big*? You never know what will hit.

He claimed that, just as the triumphs of his hits only stayed with him briefly before he moved on to the next project, he also shed the embarrassment of his failures within a few weeks. But after *Bonfire*, Hanks no longer said "yes" to every project that came down the pipeline. In fact—surprising for a man who had just made fourteen movies in just six years—he would not start a new movie for another nineteen months.

A New League

The project that lured Hanks back was *A League of Their Own*, a film about a World War II woman's baseball league directed by *Big*'s Penny Marshall. Marshall did not want Hanks for the part this time—she thought that Jimmy Dugan, an embittered alcoholic ex-player, was too sour a role for Hanks. But Hanks lobbied hard, and won her over. He gained thirty pounds for the role, the first of many weight changes he would later rue, but he enjoyed the freedom of playing "the big fat guy in the back" instead of the lead. Despite being billed behind Geena Davis, Madonna, and Rosie O'Donnell,

Hanks stole the show; the scene where he screams at a sobbing "Peaches" player (Bitty Schram) "There's no crying in baseball!" became one of the most classic bits of his whole career. The movie was a great success, making $132 million and appearing regularly in the American Film Institute's best movies list.

But Hanks's next film was an even greater hit. *Sleepless in Seattle* (1993) is an homage to the romances of Hollywood's Golden Age, taking its climax explicitly from *An Affair to Remember* (1957), starring Cary Grant. Hanks played Sam Baldwin, a widower who is coaxed by his son into talking about his loneliness and grief to a radio show host; thousands of women write in response to this discussion, and from the letters, Sam's son chooses Annie (Meg Ryan), a New Yorker, as the woman his father should meet. Hanks originally passed on the role, believing Sam to be too weak, but accepted after screenwriter Nora Ephron rewrote the script to accommodate how Hanks thought a man should act with his son.

Sleepless was released opposite the runaway blockbuster *Jurassic Park*, but despite being made for just a fraction of its rival's budget, *Sleepless* almost kept pace with it at the box office. Hanks reflected on the film's success:

It's a simple movie told within its confines and largely free of artifice. And I think audiences just responded to that. In order to enjoy most blockbuster hits these days, you've got to believe that dinosaurs can be genetically mutated, or that a guy in a batsuit can drive through a city rounding up penguins. Here, the only thing you have to believe is that two people can still fall in love.

For her part, Ephron credited the film's success to Hanks, saying that he has a rare talent as an actor to add sadness or anger to his funny scenes, or vice versa, giving his performance as the widower unusual emotional depth.

Best Actor

Hanks had a chance to tap into his full dramatic range with his next project, *Philadelphia* (1993), in which he played Andrew Beckett, gay man dying of AIDS who files a discrimination suit against his law firm. Hanks was thrilled to land such a complex role, and to work with director Jonathan Demme, just off his massive success with the serial-killer film *Silence of the Lambs* (1991). At the time, it was considered a daring role to take, since almost no box office stars had been willing to play a sympathetic gay character, much less one with AIDS. However, as an "everyday guy" in a happy, high-profile marriage, Hanks was uniquely well-suited to break these taboos without starting tabloid rumors about his personal life.

He prepped intensely for the role, losing thirty pounds and shaving his head while also reading everything he could get his hands on about the experiences of AIDS patients. He personally visited several hospitals, interviewing doctors and especially AIDS patients to understand their lives.

Hanks remembered it as a miserable and grueling time, both physically and emotionally, but the results were terrific.

Critics raved about the movie, and particularly praised Hanks for giving such a grounded, sympathetic performance of a character type that most Americans still saw as a pariah. President Bill Clinton even invited Hanks and his wife to spend the night at the White House.

The studio had held back the film for winter, so it would be released just in time for Oscar voting. No one was surprised when Hanks won the Academy Award for Best Actor, but they may have been surprised by his moving acceptance speech, in which he talked about gay friends who had influenced his life, particularly a close high school friend who had died of AIDS in 1989.

What Life is Like

In a single year, Hanks had starred in one of the most beloved romantic comedies of all time and then won a Best Actor Oscar for a different film. He had now broken out of the crowded ranks of '80s comedy stars like Steve Martin, Chevy Chase, John Candy, and Rick Moranis to become an undeniable superstar. *Forrest Gump* (1994) only continued Hanks's ascent.

Forrest Gump is the story of a mentally disabled man who has a series of incredible adventures that take him through some of the most important events of twentieth-century history. The movie has aged poorly, is rarely shown today, and is primarily remembered as having won the Best Picture Oscar, instead of the obviously more deserving *Pulp Fiction* or *Shawshank Redemption*. At the time, though, it was a smash hit, and two of its lines—"My mama always said, 'life was like a box of chocolates. You never know what you're gonna get'" and "Stupid is as stupid does"—moved permanently into pop culture. For his part, Hanks loved the script from the moment he saw it, and agreed to cut his usual salary in exchange for a share of the profits; the shrewd gamble ultimately netted him $40 million and his second consecutive Best Actor Oscar. He became the only actor since Spencer Tracy to win this award in consecutive years.

The movie was Hanks's fourth smash hit in a row, and he showed no signs of slowing down.

Back to Space

As a boy, Hanks had been obsessed with space, so Howard's *Apollo 13* (1995) was something of a dream project. The film tells the story of an ill-fated attempt by NASA to return to the moon after the Apollo 11 landing; an oxygen tank detonates, damaging the craft, and the three astronauts on board struggle to return safely to Earth. In preparing for his role, Hanks had a chance to spend several days with the mission's commander, Jim Lovell, who he plays in the film; to ride the "Vomit Comet," a training aircraft that lets passengers briefly experience weightlessness through a steep dive; and to extensively study transcripts of the real conversations between those who were on Apollo 13and the Mission Control team.

The film was critically acclaimed and a Best Picture nominee (losing to Mel Gibson's *Braveheart*). Critics had speculated that Hanks might receive his third consecutive Oscar nomination for his intense performance, but he was snubbed; after two wins in a row, Academy voters may have been suffering from some minor Hanks fatigue.

Audiences were by no means tired of Hanks, though, and *Apollo 13* did blockbuster business. By now, Hanks had become one of Hollywood's most reliable box office stars. Therefore, he could afford to take some chances, which he did by agreeing to voice Sheriff Woody, the lead in the world's first computer-animated feature film, *Toy Story* (1995). By now, Hanks had the golden touch, it seemed. Pixar's "risky" experiment proved to be another surprise hit, launching a billion-dollar franchise; as of this writing, Hanks has now voiced three movies and various shorts and specials in the series, with a fourth movie on the way.

Chapter 4:
Branching Out

Tom Hanks, Director and Producer

In just five years, Tom Hanks went from being a box office question mark to one of Hollywood's top power players. Now, he had the freedom to try some new directions: some successful, some less so.

For starters, Hanks wanted to try his hand at directing. He had long made a point of taking roles where he could have some input on the film (part of the reason his films were now of consistently higher quality). Hanks was ready to have a film all to himself.

His directorial debut *That Thing You Do!* (1996), tells the story of a fictional 1960s high school band called The Wonders, who find themselves overwhelmed by fame when their signature song suddenly becomes a nationwide hit. Hanks himself, who also wrote the film, appears briefly in the movie as Mr. White, their producer, though his motives remain suspicious and ambiguous; he manages a young singer (Tom Everett Scott) who looks uncannily like a younger version of himself. Hanks found directing far more exhausting than acting, but was reasonably satisfied with the final product. Critics had more mixed reactions, finding the result bland but occasionally charming. Hanks's only other attempt at directing to date *Larry Crowne* (2011) met with very similar reviews.

Hanks also tried his hand at producing, with much more success. Interested in retelling the stories of the astronauts that had so fascinated him as a boy, he became the executive producer of *From the Earth to the Moon* (1998), a twelve-part HBO drama series about the Apollo program. Although the series was one of the most expensive in television history at that time, it proved a massive critical and financial success, winning acclaim for its performances, accuracy, and attention to detail. In one episode, Hanks himself appears as an assistant to visionary

French film director Georges Méliès, who directed the 1902 fantasy *A Trip to the Moon*.

War and Peace

Busy with these other projects, Hanks did not star in another film until three years after *Apollo 13*. His follow-up film was the World War II blockbuster *Saving Private Ryan* (1998), Hanks's first collaboration with director Steven Spielberg. The experience was famously grueling, as Spielberg wanted the actors to go through a real boot camp to prepare for their roles. After several days of misery, the cast rebelled and took a vote to quit; only Hanks insisted on remaining. His example caused the others to reconsider, and in the end, the full cast completed boot camp together.

Hanks's character on the screen, Captain John H. Miller, was similarly inspiring, and won Hanks his fourth Best Actor nomination (he lost to Roberto Benigni for *Life Is Beautiful*). However, *Saving Private Ryan* was nominated for ten other Academy Awards, and remains highly regarded for its harrowing battle scenes, particularly the bravura depiction of the D-Day landing. The project had another real-life impact on Hanks. Shocked to discover in his research that the US had no proper memorial for World War II veterans, Hanks made an uncharacteristic foray into the political arena to lobby that a memorial be created.

As he often did, Hanks alternated a grueling project with a lighter follow-up, *You've Got Mail*. This lightweight rom-com was his third pairing with Meg Ryan, and was a remake of the comedy classic *The Shop Around the Corner*; the original had starred Jimmy Stewart, an actor to whom Hanks is often compared for their perceived modest, "everyman" qualities. The film made more than $250 million, and was praised by critics for the chemistry between its leading couple, even if the films' script was occasionally overly cute.

Two Kinds of Prisons

In 1999, Hanks teamed up with Frank Darabont, director of *The Shawshank Redemption,* to adapt *The*

Green Mile, a Steven King novel about a Depression-era prison. Hanks played head guard Paul Edgecomb, who discovers that one of his simple-minded prisoners on death row may not only be innocent but also has magical healing powers. The movie received critical acclaim, despite its 189-minute running time, and proved to be yet another box office success; Hanks had gone an astonishing full decade with all of the movies he starred in being big hits.

The following year, he took on a much more challenging role in Robert Zemeckis's *Cast Away* (2000). This film, which portrays Chuck Noland, a FedEx executive trapped on an isolated Pacific island after a plane crash, required Hanks first to gain fifty pounds to play his pre-crash character, and then to drop himself to near-starvation levels for his time on the island. As Hanks's character struggles to survive on the island, with only a volleyball ("Wilson") for companionship, the movie becomes a stunning one-man show, for which Hanks was nominated for an Academy Award for the fifth time in twelve years. Wilson also won a special award for "Best Inanimate Object" at the Critic's Choice Awards. As for the box office, the film opened with mediocre returns, but Hanks's powerhouse performance ensured that it had long legs, and the film earned more week after week; ultimately it pulled in more than $425 million.

More Experiments

Even as his acting career kept advancing, Hanks and his wife continued producing, and both with incredible success. Hanks produced *Band of Brothers* (2001), a World War II miniseries about a company of the 101st Airborne Division, which was a huge moneymaker and is still regarded as one of the best miniseries in television history. He would later return to World War II material to produce the companion piece *The Pacific* (2010), also a success. Wilson, meanwhile, took a chance on a script by comedian Nia Vardalos about her wacky family; the resulting movie, *My Big Fat Greek Wedding* (2002), was a sleeper hit of unthinkable proportions, making more than $360 million back on a $5 million budget. It remains the most profitable independent film of all time.

Hanks branched out on screen as well, taking his first major villain role since *Punchline* in Sam Mendes's *Road to Perdition* (2002). In the film, Hanks played Michael Sullivan, an ex-hit man who seeks revenge against the mobsters who killed most of his family. For a change, his semi-villainous turn was well received. The film was another hit with critics and audiences, but despite its acclaim, failed to net Hanks an expected Oscar nomination. In the same year, he played Carl Hanratty, the FBI antagonist to Leonardo DiCaprio's con man in Spielberg's *Catch Me If You Can*; the resulting film, based on a true story, was entertaining if not amazing, and proved a minor box office success. But *The Ladykillers* (2004), a remake in which Hanks played a sinister would-be murderer, was a forgettable flop—Hanks's first in a decade and a half—and he has not taken another villainous or antagonist role to date.

More successful was Hanks's second foray into computer animation, Zemeckis's *The Polar Express*

(2004). In this charming Christmas film, Hanks not only provides the voice work for six characters, but he also provided motion capture performances, then a cutting-edge technology. The film was a financial success despite its high cost, and is remembered today as a technological landmark—it is even listed in the *Guinness Book of World Records* for being the longest performance capture film. Hanks teamed up with Spielberg again in this busy year, playing a stateless refugee trapped in an airport in *The Terminal*; the film received mixed reviews for its length and relative plotlessness, but did well at the box office.

Professor and Congressman

In 2006, Hanks was tapped to play Professor Robert Langdon in the big-screen adaptation of Dan Brown's wildly popular novel, *The Da Vinci Code*. Unlike Hanks's previous experience with *Bonfire of the Vanities*, *The Da Vinci Code* proved just as popular on the big screen, and was the year's second-highest grossing film, despite poor critical reviews. The Langdon movies have proved extremely lucrative for Hanks; in 2009, he reprised the conspiracy-hunting character in *Angels & Demons* for a record $50 million plus profit sharing, the only time Hanks has done a sequel to one of his live action performances. He will appear for a third time as the character later this year (2016) in *Inferno*.

In the comedy-drama *Charlie Wilson's War* (2007), Hanks appeared opposite Julia Roberts and Philip Seymour Hoffman as troubled Texas Congressman Charlie Wilson, who led the effort to arm Afghan rebels against the Soviet occupation in the 1980s. He received a Golden Globe nomination for his role and general critical acclaim.

The Captain

Beginning in 2011, Hanks began to uncharacteristically struggle at the box office. He co-starred in *Extremely Loud and Incredibly Close* (2011) with Thomas Horn, who played Oskar Schell; Hanks played Thomas Schell, Oskar's father, who died in the World Trade Center. The film is divisive melodrama about September 11th that was loved by a few and judged as exploitive by others. The film did not do well financially, and received the dubious honor of being the only movie ever nominated for Best Picture while also being rated "Rotten" (actively disliked by a majority of critics) on the review aggregator *Rotten Tomatoes*. Hanks's next leading role was in *Cloud Atlas* (2012), which also had difficulty making back its budget. This challenging, time-jumping science fiction romance, which was based on a novel of the same name, polarized critics and audiences alike.

But Hanks soon returned to unambiguous success with *Captain Phillips* (2013), in which he portrays the title character in the true-to-life story of a ship hijacked by Somali pirates. His gritty, subtle performance shows everything that is best in Hanks's craft: his "everyman" demeanor and his ability to channel great emotional intensity. His character's descent into delirious shock after the violence of the movie's climax is a tour de force of unscripted improvisation, and one of the greatest scenes from his long career; this role won him a nomination for a Golden Globe. The same year,

Hanks also won acclaim for his role as Walt Disney in *Saving Mr. Banks*, a feel-good drama about the making of *Mary Poppins*.

New Forms

It is said that a great artist never repeats himself, and like any great artist, Hanks continued to push himself into new things. Decades after his initial stage work, he made his Broadway debut in 2013 in *Lucky Guy*, a play by Nora Ephron—his *Sleepless in Seattle* screenwriter—who had died the year before. The play tells the story of Pulitzer-winning tabloid reporter Mike McAlary, and this role won Hanks his first nomination for a Tony Award, Broadway's highest honor. In 2014, he also published a short story in *The New Yorker*, arguably the world's most prestigious literary venue, about astronaut Alan Bean, drawing once again on his deep interest in space exploration.

Meanwhile, Hanks was also making lifestyle changes. He revealed in 2013 that he had been diagnosed with type 2 diabetes and blamed a lifetime of unhealthy eating—in particular, the many roles for which he had abruptly gained or lost large amounts of weight, something he said he would no longer do for his films.

But no matter what other changes he made, Hanks's first love would always be film work. In 2015, he teamed up with Spielberg for the fourth time in *Bridge of Spies*, a Cold War thriller. Hanks plays real-life lawyer James Donovan, who seeks to defuse international tensions by arranging a swap of a captured KGB colonel and downed American U-2 pilot Gary Powers. The film is a paean to the power of everyday decency to make the world a better place, and unsurprisingly makes an ideal vehicle for Hanks, who received widespread praise for his part.

The Future

Despite his illness and advancing age, Hanks shows no signs of slowing down. He has now been appearing in hit films for more than three decades, making him the fourth highest-grossing Hollywood actor in history. It should be noted that two of the actors on the list ahead of him, Samuel L. Jackson and Morgan Freeman, are there only by virtue of appearing as *supporting* characters in successful films; only Harrison Ford, the top name, can really compete with Hanks as a leading man.

Even at the time of this writing, Hanks has several films in production that are almost certain to be hits: *Sully* (2016), the Clint Eastwood-directed story of the pilot who performed the "Miracle Landing" on the Hudson River; *Inferno* (2016), the newest Robert Langdon thriller; *The Circle* (2016), a science-fiction drama with *Harry Potter* star Emma Watson; and a fourth *Toy Story* (2018) film. Although he resists the comparison, Hanks has indisputably joined the ranks of all-time stars like Jimmy Stewart and Cary Grant and has taken a permanent place in the Hollywood firmament.

Sources

"Biography - Tom Hanks: The Luckiest Man in the World." A&E Home Video, 2007.

Gardner, David. *Tom Hanks: The Unauthorized Biography*. London: Blake, 1999.

Kramer, Barbara. *People to Know: Tom Hanks*. Berkeley Heights, NJ: Enslow, 2001.

"List of Tom Hanks Performances." *Wikipedia*. Accessed 2 Sept. 2016.

Marshall, Penny. "*My Mother Was Nuts* Book Excerpt: How Robert De Niro, Not Tom Hanks, Almost Starred In Penny Marshall's *Big*." *Movieline*, 18 Sept. 2012. Accessed 2 Sept. 2016.

Pockross, Adam. "No Piano? No Problem! *Big* Revelations from Director Penny Marshall." *Yahoo Movies*, 11 Dec. 2013. Accessed 2 Sept. 2016.

"*Splash*." *Wikipedia*. Accessed 2 Sept. 2016.